THE LIGHT OF ZARATHUSTRA

The Story of the World's First Prophet of Light

BB Sage

THE LIGHT OF ZARATHUSTRA

Stories from the Zoroastrian Faith

This book is published by The Crackajack Company under the Brainy Bubs imprint. Brainy Bubs creates books that introduce children to cultures, wisdom traditions, and great ideas from around the world in a simple and engaging way.

Author B.B. Sage

First published in 2026

ISBN Hardcover 978-81-69067-38-6

ISBN Paperback 978-81-69067-17-1

This book introduces young readers to stories and teachings associated with the ancient Zoroastrian tradition, one of the world's oldest spiritual paths.

For every child who has ever watched a candle flame and wondered where the light comes from.

One Love, Many Paths

A Brainy Bubs Book

Ages 3+

A long, long time ago - longer ago than you can imagine - a baby was born in the land of ancient Persia.
That land is now called Iran.

The moment he was born, they say, the baby laughed.
Not cried. Laughed.
As if he already knew something wonderful that the rest of the world had yet to discover.

His parents named him Zarathustra.
Say it slowly: Zah – rah – THOO – strah.

And this is his story.

Zarathustra grew up surrounded by fields and rivers and animals and sky.
He loved all of it deeply.

But even as a small boy, he asked big questions.
Why do people hurt each other?
Why is there cruelty in the world?
Who made the sun, the stars, the wind, the rain?
Is there a God? And if there is - what does God want from us?

His questions were so big
that sometimes he would sit quietly for hours, just thinking.

Zarathustra grew into a young man.

He studied. He prayed. He searched.
He lived simply and honestly.
He was kind to animals and gentle with people.

But the questions never went away.

Why is there good in the world?
Why is there evil?
Which one is stronger?
Which one will win?

He needed to find out. So he went searching.

For years, Zarathustra wandered and
prayed and wondered.

He was about thirty years old
when something extraordinary happened.

He had gone to a river at dawn
to draw water for a sacred ceremony.

As he stepped into the cold water,
he saw a shining being standing on the
riverbank.

The being glowed like the sun itself.

Zarathustra could barely look at him.
But he was not afraid.

The shining being spoke.

"I am Vohu Manah," he said. "Good Mind."
"Come with me."

Zarathustra followed.

And there, in a great vision of light, he came before Ahura Mazda - the Lord of Wisdom.
The one God.

The God of light, of truth, of everything good.

Zarathustra had found his answer.

HUMATA. HUKHTA. HVARSHTA

Ahura Mazda spoke to Zarathustra.

Not with thunder. Not with fear.
But with warmth - like sunlight caressing your face.

"There is good in the world and there is darkness," Ahura Mazda said. "Every person must choose between them."

"Choose good thoughts.
Speak good words.
Do good deeds."

Three simple things.
And the light will always win.

Zarathustra came back from his vision completely changed.

He had met God.

He had been given a message for all of humanity.

Now he had to share it.

He went home to his family first.

His cousin Maidhyoimanha was the first person to believe his story.

Every great teacher needs one person who believes in them first.

But not everyone listened.
The priests of the old religion were angry.

They worshipped many gods.
They did not like Zarathustra's new message:
one God, one truth,
one simple choice between good and evil. They drove him away.

For years, Zarathustra wandered from place to place, sharing his message wherever he went. Some people listened. Most did not.

He was lonely. But he did not give up.

For ten long years, Zarathustra searched for someone to believe him.

Ten years is a very long time to wait.

But Zarathustra believed that truth is always worth waiting for.

Then one day, he arrived at the court of a great king.
The king's name was Vishtaspa.
He was wise and fair and curious.

Zarathustra asked for two days to share his message. King Vishtaspa said yes.

Zarathustra spoke to the king and his court about Ahura Mazda -the God of wisdom and light.

He spoke about the three great rules:

Good Thoughts. Good Words. Good Deeds.

He spoke about truth - Asha -
the invisible force that holds the whole universe together.

He spoke about how every person,
no matter how small or how young,
has the power to choose the light.

The king listened to every single word.

King Vishtaspa believed him.
He became the first great royal follower of Zarathustra.

With the king's support, Zarathustra could finally share his message openly.

People came from near and far to listen. The message was simple enough for a child to understand and deep enough for a wise person to spend a lifetime exploring.

Good Thoughts.
Good Words.
Good Deeds.

Three rules. One flame.

And it was spreading.

Zarathustra also taught people to honor the world around them.

The earth is sacred, he said. Do not poison it.

The water is sacred. Do not dirty it.

The air is sacred. Do not foul it.

And fire - beautiful, warm, life-giving fire -
is the most sacred symbol of all.

Not a god to worship. But a reminder.
A reminder that God is here.

Warm. Real. Close.

Zarathustra's teachings were written down in a sacred book called the Avesta.

The oldest and most beautiful part is called the Gathas -seventeen hymns that Zarathustra wrote himself.

They are among the oldest writings in all of human history.
Older than most of the Bible.
Older than the Quran.

In them, Zarathustra asks questions, wonders aloud, and speaks directly to God - like a friend talking to a friend.

Zarathustra lived a long life.
He married and had children.
He laughed and ate and slept and
woke like any other human being.
But his message was not like any
other message.

It travelled far beyond him.
It crossed mountains and deserts
and seas. It touched the hearts of
kings and farmers and children.

Long after Zarathustra was gone,
his flame kept burning.

One of the greatest kings who ever lived
was a Zoroastrian - a follower of
Zarathustra.

His name was Cyrus the Great.

When Cyrus conquered new lands,
he did not make people slaves.

He let them go home.

He let them keep their own religions.
He let them live in peace.

He wrote this down on a clay tablet -
the world's very first human
rights charter.

Thousands of years passed.

Empires rose and fell.

New religions came into the world.

But Zarathustra's flame did not go out. His followers kept it alive - carefully, lovingly, passing it from hand to hand, generation to generation.

Some of them had to leave their home to keep the flame safe. They sailed across a great sea to a land that would welcome them.

That land was India.

The people who brought the sacred flame from Iran to India are called the Parsis - people from Persia.

They were welcomed with open arms. They blended into their new home with grace and joy, and they kept their sacred fire burning.

The sacred flame first came to India more than a thousand years ago.

Today it burns in the town of Udvada, where it has been carefully kept alive for nearly three hundred years.

Without ever going out.

CANADA
IRAN
U.S.A.
INDIA
AUSTRALIA
FEWER THAN 200,000 PEOPLE
THE BIGGEST SMALL FLAME IN THE WORLD

Today, the followers of Zarathustra are called Zoroastrians. There are not many of them in the world -fewer than two hundred thousand.

But their light has touched billions of lives. The ideas of one God, of heaven and earth, of angels, of the final victory of good over evil -all of these were in Zarathustra's teachings first, thousands of years before anyone else wrote them down.

He was, perhaps, the world's first prophet of light.

CYRUS THE GREAT
CYRUS THE GREAT
FREDDIE MERCURY
FREDDIE MERCURY
HOMI BHABHA
E = mc²
HOMI BHABHA
RATAN TATA
RATAN TATA
ZUBIN MEHTA
ZUBIN MEHTA
THE CONNECTING FLAME
'FIVE PILLARS OF LIGHT'

Some of the most remarkable people in the world have carried Zarathustra's flame.

A king who freed enslaved people.
A scientist who built India's first nuclear reactor.
A conductor who made music across the entire globe.
A businessman who gave his fortune to the poor.
A singer whose voice shook stadiums of a hundred thousand people.

All of them Zoroastrians.

All of them living by the same three rules:

Good Thoughts. Good Words. Good Deeds.

Try noticing your thoughts
today.
Are they kind?

Try speaking honestly-
even if your voice shakes a
little.

Try doing one small, good
thing.

That's enough.

It always has been.

Good Thoughts.
Good Words.
Good Deeds.

The flame is yours now.

Carry the light forward.

A Little More About Zarathustra

Zarathustra (also known as Zoroaster in Greek) lived in ancient Persia more than 3,000 years ago. Scholars believe he was born sometime between 1500 BCE and 600 BCE. His exact dates remain uncertain, which only adds to his mystery. The religion he founded, Zoroastrianism, is believed to be one of the world's earliest monotheistic faiths - teaching belief in one supreme God.

Many ideas that later appear in Judaism, Christianity, and Islam -such as heaven and hell, angels, free will, and the ultimate triumph of good over evil - were already present in Zarathustra's teachings.

The word Zoroastrian comes from the Greek form of Zarathustra's name. His followers in India, who arrived from Persia about 1,400 years ago, are called Parsis — from the word Pars, meaning Persia.
Today there are fewer than 200,000 Zoroastrians in the world, yet their contribution to human history has been remarkable. Their central teaching remains beautifully simple:

Humata — Good Thoughts
Hukhta — Good Words
Hvarshta — Good Deeds

These ideas have endured for more than three thousand years and remain as powerful today as they were when Zarathustra first taught them.

More Books in the One Love, Many Paths Series

Available Now

The 99 Names of Allah — Islam

The Hindu Gods and Goddesses — Hinduism

Coming Soon

The Teachings of the Sikh Gurus - Sikhism

The Fifteen Faces of the Buddha - Buddhism

Jesus Loves Children - Christianity

Shabbat, Tikkun Olam and the Talmud - Judaism

Mahavira and the Sacred Path - Jainism

All titles are also available with companion coloring books.

Brainy Bubs

Where learning meets light.

Printed at Repro India Ltd.